I
Was
Busy
Surviving

Christina L. John

B K
ROYSTON
Publishing

BK Royston Publishing
P. O. Box 4321
Jeffersonville, IN 47131
http://www.bkroystonpublishing.com
bkroystonpublishing@gmail.com

Cover Design: Elite Book Covers

ISBN-13: 978-1-963136-38-8

Printed in the United States of America

Dedication

For My Husband:

Your unwavering love changed the course

of my life forever

Acknowledgements

To my parents, without your love, resiliency, and support, I wouldn't be the person I am today.

A special thanks to my best girlfriends, Allison, Casie, Aleah, and Celeste, who have lived these stories with me, in real time. Who loved when I couldn't love myself and encouraged me to share my words with the world.

And to Tabitha, Why Not Us?

Table of Contents

Introduction

In her debut novel "I Was Busy Surviving" Christina John walks us through her reckoning of generational poverty, self-sabotage, betrayal, accepting love, and the day-to-day emotions that lead and guide our decisions. Capitalizing on the raw emotion and challenges that we face every day, but rarely say out loud, I Was Busy Surviving targets those are still in this journey and give hope that you can break generational chains and begin living life to its fullest.

Divided into sections titled Surviving, Existing, Drowning, Living and Thriving, Christina writes "I see a world above me and one below me / I'm stuck in this space where I'm merely a bystander / not actively living in either / I watch two lives run parallel / neither make sense, so I stay in this world" as a reminder that we all get lost and find ourselves as a bystander in our lives but we can all overcome this with self-awareness and accepting love.

Surviving

I asked my mind one time, exactly what is it you want me to say?

And the words haven't stopped spilling onto these pages since.

Late Fees

Insufficient fund fees

Reactivation fees

Bank fees

It cost money to be this poor.

Cash advances

Student loans

Lottery tickets

Personal loans

It cost money to be this hopeful

Payment plans

Interest rates

Renting

Lay-a-away

It costs money to be resourceful.

Double Shifts

Cigarettes

Broken bodies

Broken minds

It cost more than money to be this poor

When someone asks, "Why can't they
figure it out?"
It's because we are suffocated by the costs

I went to a school across town

It was the promised land for someone like me;

I was considered lucky to even set in

I was supposed to be grateful for the opportunity

Girls of my status, don't get to come here

This school is my way out

I knew what my mom was doing,

she was trying to help

She wanted me to find people like me,

since I wasn't like them

When I arrived, I immediately knew

something was off

I was from the wrong side of the tracks

Instinct told me to lie about where we lived

What my parents did for a living

And where I bought my clothes

I was a loner in navigating what felt like

a vast landscape

A wilderness with thick trees and a food chain

A food chain I was at the bottom of

Unless I learned to walk, talk, and dress like them
I knew I needed to fit in, standing out was painful
The girls traveled in packs.
They had been friends forever

I became painfully aware of how different I was
These girls spared no effort in telling me
I felt their words, looks and actions
With their sharp teeth,
they bit into an already damaged soul
Everyone saw potential and
I saw them as the wolves they were
Devouring anything that was different

I carried my mother's burdens. She laid them on me
unwillingly and unknowingly
I knew things I shouldn't have known.
Who else was she going to tell?
After all, I was also her best friend

I tried to lighten her load; I really did
I did all the things she wanted me to do
But she wasn't ready to let go of them
Now they have become her identity
What would she do without them?
The weight never seemed to bother her
the way it did me

It's time to lay these down
They were too heavy
And I had carried them far too long

It was as if the holes in these walls were
more than just a memento

He left keeping us on edge and never repaired them
They served as constant reminders of our poverty
We couldn't escape it,
Even the walls told us so

I ask you, "Have you ever seen

blue-collar strength?"

The physicality that grows crops

Drives trucks

Works on machinery

And moves mountains

Have built homes, motors, and roads

They hold everything together with their paychecks

The costs are their broken bodies

Their children have seen them work

from sun up to sun down

Day in and day out

All in the name of providing

They are admired by those who love them

Looked down on by those who need them

And wanted by those who make money off them

But what's on the inside is broken beyond repair

Like Humpty Dumpty,

they cannot be put together again

The juxtaposition of strength and brokenness that

can be found,

Side by side, living in a single person

The one thing they can't fix is themselves.

I hear people describe their mothers as kind,

Loving, generous, virtuous, and beautiful

My mother has all these attributes

Most importantly, she's the strongest person I know

Strong is often a word used to describe fathers

But because of our father's odd jobs, she was our
mother and father

She was enforcer, provider, our true north

The one person who kept it all together

Even when it was all falling apart

I'll never understand

how she would always pull it off

But she did

Every time

And we love her all the more for it

I went to a sleepover last night

They had two bathrooms in their house

Their dad made pancakes for us the next morning

My friend had her own room

separate from her sister.

We could shut the door and listen to CDs

There weren't any holes in the floors or walls

I didn't notice a basement that was wet or

smelled like mold

I wasn't asked to put wood in the stove

I remember thinking over and over again

Their dad must work at the FORD plant.

Not construction like mine

It rained two days last week, and he didn't work

We knew better than to ask for anything this week

His check was short

You call yourself an empath

When you are really a sociopath

You don't actually love anyone

It's not something you are capable of

No contact is usually best

It's the only way I can remember

Who you really are

I know you see these scars

They are visible

Out in the open for the world to see

I've tried to cover them

But they are woven into the fabric of my being

I always thought these scars were invisible

Since the cuts were deep inside me

Turns out, everyone could see them but me

I know when people see them

They wonder, "Who hurt you?"

I wish I had a direct answer

One that wouldn't lead to more questions

Who did hurt me?

Was it my father with his affairs and lies?

Was it my mother who should have left?

Was it poverty and survival of the fittest?

Was it society?

Or was it how they failed the poor,

the women, the fragile?

Who did hurt me?

The answer has always been clear

I hurt myself, more than anyone ever could

But the beautiful thing about scars is

Eventually they no longer hurt

They just get filled in with years of scar tissue,

making them numb

So, while I know you see them

Don't feel sorry for me

I promise…they no longer hurt

I see you hide your hands

They aren't small

Nor fragile

Or petite

They aren't feminine or delicate

You have your dad's hands

Masculine and rough

But those hands held us all together

When it all fell apart

They planted gardens every spring

They nursed us each back to health

Those hands helped Dad in the shop

Mowed grass

Cut wood

Those hands did homework and class projects

Cooked dinner

Tended the yard

Mama, these hands aren't what you want them to be

But they are everything to me

Is this the life you envisioned?

Envisioned

What a peculiar word

Dreamed

Wanted

Manifested

Are those words synonymous with envision?

Is envision a verb?

A noun?

Can you be more specific?

Can you use it in a sentence?

See, I can't understand how one envisions the future

when all they can see is the past

Surviving isn't a life filled with dreams and hopes

It is a life filled with reactions and calculations

Calculating the costs of the next move

Envisioning is a luxury that survivors can't afford

It's too expensive

Disappointment would fall too heavy on already
burdened laid shoulders
We are taught not to add to the existing
weight we carry
Just
One hour
One day
One week
One month at a time

I never envisioned this life
I was too busy surviving it

As much as our mother tried

You just wouldn't listen

She wanted you to break our curse

But you weren't aware enough of one to break it.

You made yourself at home, nice and cozy making
choices that lead to a chaotic life.

A life that felt normal on the inside but from the
outside was anything but

We've been told you were the "strong one"

Evidently not strong enough to be the example

I needed you to be

When I needed to see a way out,

you couldn't provide that

So I made my own

They have a name for it now,
it's called parentification.

There was no name for it back then.

We were too young to be your best friends

You should have had your own

Why didn't you have any?

What kept you from having friends?

You were emotionally relying on us,
and it was too much

I was raising myself; I couldn't raise you too

I don't blame you for staying

You had no income, no resources

And

Three mouths to feed

But, could you have imagined a life where you left?

A life that could have taken us places

Away from poverty

Away from the lies

Away from the anger

Away from it all

But alas, patterns repeat themselves

And even if you left, we would find ourselves back

where we started

You can't outrun your destiny

It has a way of hunting you down

My mom was great at math

She knew exactly how many days it would take the grocery store to clear her bounced check

She knew how to make a dollar stretch as far as it could possibly go

She knew adding macaroni to any dish possible filled us up faster and longer
She knew it was $2.15 in gas because you also needed a pack of Misty Lights.
She knew which bills could be late
and the ones that couldn't.

She knew to pay the water bill at the grocery on the same day to have the service turned back on before Dad got home.

She knew where to always find loose change underneath the seats in the truck.

My mother made things add up when they absolutely shouldn't have been able to.

He never drank alcohol

When he punched a hole in our wall

He never drank alcohol

When he pushed Mama against the stove

He never drank alcohol

When he pointed a gun at her and him

He never drank alcohol

When he ripped the phone from the wall

He never drank alcohol

When his mistress told us all

He never drank alcohol

When his temper raged

He never drank alcohol

Because he saw his father drink too much

He never drank alcohol

When he was ruining our lives

He never drank alcohol

He didn't have to

In order to have his demons on display

For the longest time, I decided to accept an apology
that was never said.
I knew you were sorry. I could tell by the way you
were showing up
I knew you were sorry because I could tell you were
softer now

When in reality,
I think you just grew older with age
The temper subsided, and you settled down
I don't actually think you are sorry,
and you never will be

Once I realized this, I could begin to heal
I was no longer twisting reality and started
accepting it for what It was
I can work with reality, what I know to be true.
What I couldn't work with was the fantasy
I had in my mind
That of an apologetic man

I'm sorry that you're not sorry

The only way I can move forward,

Is knowing that you're not

Do you have mental illness,
or do you just have trauma?

Our mother enabled you,
and our father hardened you.
I see how this could affect you.

You've tried to medicate it away still, it lingers

But you were so young when they fought the most.
There is no way you remember it like me
How much do you actually remember?

We stay on edge, waiting for your next episode.
I can't remember the last time I heard you laugh
A laugh from deep inside of you
The medication has taken that away

Anxiety is a symptom, a part of a whole.
There is a much bigger picture
I wish you could see it as clearly as I do

You aren't as broken as you think.

It's not your fault. I'm sorry

I've watched my childhood best friend

become his own worst enemy

It's an ordinary experience for most people,

some only dread the chore of it

I know it's anxiety inducing for some,

but it's a necessity of life for all

A common denominator

An equalizer if you will

But it's not an equalizer

Is it?

We all know that

Some people can blissfully get whatever

they want and need

Most people can only get what they need

A few can't even get that

All walks of age, color, and economic status

Walking past each other

Only those who struggle notice the ones who don't

I can see my mom's anxiety

as she stands by the cashier

Watching the register add up the total

With the scan of each item, anxiety grows

Take off two items

Add one back

Replace it with this one

The mental math is exhausting

Her anxiety has now spilled over on to me

I watch her count dollars and exact change

Struggling to get all the needed items

to feed us this week

What should be a normal trip to the grocery store

Is the worst day of the week for some

I saw him for what he wasn't

He wasn't kind

He wasn't gentle

He wasn't nurturing

He wasn't loyal

He wasn't a provider

He wasn't a protector

He wasn't a father

How do you not hear them?

They are everywhere.

In the walls

In the cabinets

All over the floor

Under the fridge

My memories can be dated by them

When they entered

And by the time they left

Checking my backpack

Checking our food

Never allowed to have friends over

How do you not hear them? Or are you pretending?

Because acknowledging how loud they are

Would require more than you can handle

How am I the only one who hears them?

Because to me…

The noise these roaches make

Is deafening

I see my friends spend time with their families

They go vacations together

They go shopping, dinner, parties

Instantly feel envious

Just the site of families being together

Do you enjoy your family

enough to vacation with them?

I wish I did too

But what if I don't like mine?

What happens if you don't fit in and never did?

They knew it, I knew it

I know I am supposed to love them

And I do

But it's so complicated, we are so complicated

We are so different—each one of us

In another world, our paths wouldn't even cross

The only thing we have in common is our parents

So, we keep in touch—for them.

For our kids to have cousins

We play pretend at Christmas and birthdays

We love our mom, and for now, that connects us

Facebook Post: June 16, 2019

Happy Father's Day, Buttermilk Bob.
Thanks for teaching me all the important things in life such as: How to tell the difference between Clint Eastwood westerns, all the sockets by size, how to make you a pot of coffee at age five, how to drive a backhoe well before I should have, what company makes the best heavy equipment, how to net crawdads and how to jug ponds for the biggest snapper turtles.

Honorable mention lessons: How to drive a '78 Ford Bronco down the Outer Loop alone at age twelve, how to load a stove with pieces of wood so it can keep the house warm all night, always telling me directions by east and west instead of left or right, and every injury really 'isn't that bad' (even with bone visible and seven stitches needed).

Also, a major shout-out for saving me thousands of dollars in car repairs over the years. I love you,

Dad, despite your breaking every child labor law that ever existed.

Existing

Of all the haunted places I've been

Nothing is more haunting than being left alone with

my thoughts

"Are you still here?" Asked the computer screen

"Yes, I am still here; I just got distracted," I replied.

When in fact, this is what my headstone should read

I get lost in the depths of this life

The dimensions are plentiful

And I can't keep track of the ones I have entered

The ones that should stay closed

And the ones that should stay open

I live in a space of redirection

Opening and closing doors until a path is

laid out in front of me

One that keeps the dark dimensions sealed

and the light open

"If I marry you, I marry your student loans.

And then I put you through college, and for what?"

An ex-boyfriend explaining to me

why he broke up with me

Isn't it ironic they are called social networks?

When, in reality, they are isolating
us from each other

I find it strange I know so much about a stranger but
not my own sister

We are biologically made to crave connection, but
not the dial-up kind

We need human touch, human embrace.

Not a Facetime call

I want to hug you.

The habits we have picked up fill our voids, using
screens to keep our minds busy.

Heaven forbid, we allow our brain to relax,
our thoughts to wander.

We think we are connected, but we have never been
more disconnected in human history

Nothing tastes as good as being bitter feels.

I've been told I have a way with words

Which is confusing because I have also been told
that I need to be quiet

Which is it?

Do you want to hear what I have to say, or do you
want me to be silent?
You can't have it both ways

Indecision weighs more heavily than the actual decision.

I have positioned myself in a place that is neither
heaven nor hell

The only way to free myself from this purgatory

I put myself into is to love myself

Unapologetically

Only then will I be free to be authentic

Without worry, judgement, or control

Loving myself will lead me to living

Actually living, a concept that is new to me

But I'm fighting for it every day

How did I end up the villain in this story?

When I've always been the hero.

When did I stop fighting and accept my fate?

Villains aren't made by circumstance

They are born

This person was always there

Being the hero was exhausting

Draining on the very soul I was trying to protect,

The hero was noble and bold

But the villain was easy and more successful

How does one find the strength to

keep up with hero work

To keep saving someone

who doesn't want to be saved?

Journal Entry: August 2021

You mentioned you wished I acted more excited to see you when you get home. Immediately, I replied that I was sorry and would work on it. You replied with, "Its ok, it's just not who you are."

Correct. It just isn't who I am. I keep thinking about why. Why do I not greet my husband each day happily, warmly, and with a kiss. I do not greet him angrily or in a bad mood, but it isn't over the top loving either.

Then it hits me because usually when the dad comes home, complete chaos ensues.

I'm sorry if it feels like I draw back and retreat from
this life we have created
You pull me back in every time
It's instinctual for you at this point

You know the signs to look for
When I start to wonder and go adrift
You gear up for the battle that is set to come
And fight whatever demons I let rise to the surface

I often wonder
Is your armor getting too heavy and worn
The constant suiting up, taking hits
It must wear on the metal

You never show it
If you are tired or if the armor is getting weak
You remain steady and true
Even when I do not understand why

I never asked you to fight these battles

But I am grateful that you do

Otherwise, I'd lose this war

Have you tried turning it off and back on again?

Me wondering if this would work in life.

I can see how the dominos had to fall this way

I know I put them into motion years ago

Bone by bone, I made these choices

I set them all up and watched them fall

But why are they still falling?

I should be able to stand them upright

Start over with a new pattern

One with clean lines and sharp turns

This old pattern still falls, and I can't stop it

What force is needed to stop these objects in motion

I need more than just my will to make them stop

I need strength to begin anew

This feels right

A storm waiting right outside my door

I've been waiting for it and it waiting for me

My soul craves the chaos it will bring

I feel lost without it

The only way I know how to go on,

Is when everything is spiraling

The uncertainty

The survival

The rush that floods my brain

I am not sure how much longer

I can keep the door closed

My ears ring with this calmness

I search for more noise

I have to open the door

It's the only way to quiet my demons

I see a world above me and one below me

I'm stuck in this space where I'm merely a bystander

Not actively living in either

I watch two lives running parallel

Neither makes sense, so I'll stay in this world

The one I created only for me

With the thoughts in my head that I can't say aloud

Which world will have

the greatest force to pull me in?

Which world wants me more?

Which world will I feel alive in?

The space between is where I will stay

From here, at least, I have both of you

Drowning

I have spiraled beyond any control, and it's the first time I have felt alive in years.

His touch burned my skin

It was forbidden, yet so welcomed

I anticipated it for months

What would it feel like if he just touched me?

It burned my skin in a way

I could still feel him on me hours after he was gone

His touch turned my stomach in so many ways

For all the right reasons

And all the wrong reasons

The grasp so tight, that my throat closed

If I had words, they could not escape

I surrendered to the flames, they engulfed me,

I could no longer fight them

Slowly turning me into ashes

By the time he kissed me, I was already scorched

earth no one would walk upon

I couldn't see a way out

There was no water for relief

No one was willing to put out these flames

He pulled me so far down into the depths of his hell

no one would save me

I'm sorry, it still hurts, I know it does.

I tend to brush off your pain because I know

I'm the one who caused it

It can be exhausting on my system,

Knowing all these years later,

I'm still causing pain from my actions years ago

I'm still paying for it professionally and personally

At times, I want to scream,

"Haven't I paid enough!"

But the answer is betrayal like that

I'm going to pay forever

Our therapists ordered no sex during this time, I couldn't have been more relieved.

Now, I don't have to hide the fact that I am thinking about him while you're fucking me.

My mind often drifts to a made-up world, one where we can be together. One where we found each other much earlier. One where you aren't my boss, and we aren't married to someone else.

If your heart and mind are disagreeing,
always trust your mind.
Your heart likes to play tricks on you.
A game it likes to play.

If I am called a mistress, what are you called?

Why doesn't society have a name for you also?

An equal partner in this destruction deserves an equal name.

This all seems unfair.

What should they call a man who crossed the line,

or a married man who has done this before?

Why do I have a name and you don't?

I need a name for you,

one that sounds as harsh as mine.

I need society to decide what you should be called.

Because right now,

the only name I have for you is my soulmate

My husband asked me if I loved you

It was out of the blue; he was standing at the sink.

At that moment, I couldn't think fast enough;

it was dizzying.

Invisible hands were choking me, unable to speak

If I hesitated any longer, he would know I was lying

I didn't lie this time

I told him the truth

I told him I thought I loved you at one point.

But I knew it wasn't love.

I knew it wasn't getting through the mundane,

day-to-day kind of love.

That kind of love doesn't last

It's a flashpoint built on chaos and dopamine

Surely to combust as quickly as it started

with no staying properties

The love I have is good, steadfast, and lasting

The kind of love that holds true in the middle of

night the same as it does in the daylight

The kind of love that I am going to hold on to

I know you have forgiven me, but I also know that you haven't forgotten either. I will spend the rest of my life trying to make sure you forget what I put you through.

My mom stayed.

Her mom stayed.

Her sister stayed.

My sister stayed.

You stayed.

What other option was there?

You saw the parts of me my father broke because
your father broke those parts too

You saw the parts of me that poverty took because
poverty took that away from you

You saw the pieces of my scattered mind
Because you've spent years
trying to piece yours together

You could understand the parts of
me that no one else could
For the first time, I was not just seen,
I was understood

But we all know that broken pieces are
hard to put back together
Two parts don't always make a whole

And for that, we could never be together

We could never make each other complete

We can only do that ourselves

And well, we all know that you never will

Journal Entry:

Wednesday, June, 2021

In therapy we discussed what "no contact" with him would look like and how it would help. Am I just supposed to forget that I felt like someone else was my soulmate?

Are you just supposed to settle and focus on what's in front of you? I can't focus on a single thing. My mind is racing and blank all at once. I'm still drifting between stories made up in my head and the reality of what's in front of me.

What is going on? How do I stop this? Maybe no contact is the only answer?

You told me you fucked your wife differently in those exact words.

Sitting at your desk, In your suit, in the most inappropriate of places.

I wasn't exactly sure what that meant,

But the rush that went through my body made me want to jump out of my skin

My thoughts raced, my face burned with desire and embarrassment.

And I just sat there
I still couldn't believe I was here
In this place so disconnected from
my myself and my marriage
I was numb
It's not me living this chaotic life that
I spent years trying to calm
It wasn't me, sitting there caught up in his charm
I still wonder who that girl was sitting there
because I know
It wasn't me
I don't know her

Certainly, if I saw her today,

I wouldn't even recognize her

I often think of the snake, that even when it sheds its skin, it's still a snake.

It was a slow burn

I can't tell you the exact moment

I saw you differently

But one day, here we are

Going down in flames together

Lotus

The only way I know how to externalize this
internal pain is by these piercing needles
Each week for hours, I allow him to drag these
colors across my back in winching pain
As if, this is my penance for the pain
I've caused others

There is no other remedy for this
Only the body can keep score
My body, therefore, must pay for the damage that
my mind has caused

I wear these flowers like a badge of honor
I wear these flowers as a reminder
I wear these flowers on my back,
like the Scarlett Letter that they are

I was warned about you

You've done this before
But like a moth to a flame
I was instantly drawn to you

To your voice
To your intelligence
To your light eyes
To your smile, my god, your smile

I couldn't stop what was happening
I was already caught in your web the first time
I met you

We are playing a dangerous game

One where everybody loses and no one wins

Yet, we are both determined to win this losing game

Journal Entry:

Friday May 21, 2021

I picked up my son from school today. He was
carrying a drawing of our family, all four of us.
I cried on the way home; I don't think he noticed.
How could I not keep our family together?
What am I doing?

Music connected us

When I want to be close to you, I put on the music
we shared.

I hope *you* are listening to it at the same time
As if the wavelengths could find you and
speak to *you*
Tell *you* that I am still thinking about *you*

Yell at me

Scream at me

Say out loud all the things I did to you

Tell me I'm a monster and how much you hate me

Remind me

that you would never do this to someone you love

Go ahead and leave

Find someone who deserves you

But for the love of God, just don't be kind to me

Every night we sit on this porch

Inhaling these cigarettes, hoping to take the edge off

Even if temporary, we are desperate for relief

From this anxiety

I'm lying, you know I'm lying.

We leave it all unsaid

We both look out to the street, not to each other

And take another long drag

Searching for the truth

But the truth is too painful to say out loud

It's too overwhelming and these cigarettes

aren't fooling anyone

Their relief lasts only for a moment

And what we need to say,

those words would last a lifetime

We are going to be ok

I'm going to come back to you.

I'm just temporarily losing my mind

Just let me work through this

Give me space

I'm feeling suffocated—I can't breathe

Don't ask questions

you don't want to know the answer to

Because I don't know the answers either.

I don't know why I am destroying the only good

thing to happen to me.

Perhaps, it is because I've held it together my entire

life, and I'm so tired.

I'm losing my grip on what I've fought to get:

the degrees, the job, the marriage, the kids.

It's just all too much.

Can you do me a favor?

Can you pick up the fight for a while?

Can you take it where I left off?

Let me lay on this bathroom floor a bit longer.

I promise I'm coming back;

I think I just finally lost myself

Wasn't it bound to happen?

No one can hold on this tight for this long

Living

How to fix a child with anxiety:

Fix the mother first.

Am I a hard pill to swallow,

or do you just want me smaller

Smaller so you can swallow me more easily,

with less discomfort

A dose of me easier to digest into

something your stomach can handle

We all know you get to decide

I don't get a say in how you take me

So, tell me, do you need to break me in half first

Or can you handle all of me at once?

Don't I Wish I Could Be Barbie?

Not because pink is my favorite color
Or her perfect hair
Ideal measurements
Impressive wardrobe
It isn't because she is a billionaire
Or the fact that she has a Ken
Malibu dreamhouse
or a convertible

It is because she can be whatever she wants to be
She doesn't have a vagina

You hired me because of my intelligence, ethics, and leadership.

You fired me because you weren't ready to find these attributes in a woman.

I can dovetail onto what you are saying

I know how to pivot in a conversation

I can circle back with the best of them

I know to deep dive into deliverables

I send out action items, core competencies,

and ratings

I am putting out fires all day long

I grab all the low-hanging fruit

Even though I wear high heels and skirts,

just as I'm instructed

I am constantly told to put a pin in it

You move the goalpost when I'm too close

All my bosses have hard stops when I'm speaking

Never hesitating to throw me under the bus

When I speak up, I'm told to take it offline

I'm always the one out of pocket, never in line

Per my last email, I will not be silent,

I will not go away

I know my worth

I know my place

I will continue to run my ideas up the flagpole until
you decide they stick
I'm constantly evaluating my bandwidth
And the last time I checked,
I withstand more than you

I don't need your love, time, or money
I tried to obtain all three at
different points for different reasons
And I failed miserably at each attempt

Don't worry
I still got the best part of you
He's kind, considerate and thoughtful
He's full of forgiveness

He's generous with his love and affection
He doesn't keep score or tally up costs
He gives more than he takes

Maybe I didn't get the best part of you because I
have never seen those parts of you
He became everything you never gave him.

He's the best part of me
Back home
Waiting with the life that we made for ourselves
Without any help from you

And maybe for tonight, you remind yourself of all the things you are doing right. Maybe focus less on where you think you fall short and more on where you show up. We were never meant to carry all this weight, let some of it go. Be light, be confident, laugh again, and laugh more... you are doing so much right, don't focus on what you think you are doing wrong. You wouldn't be human if you were perfect, but you aren't broken as much as you think.

Poverty steals your personality

You have to take it back forcefully,

one decision at a time

When you are coming out of surviving,

it can feel overwhelming

It feels silly, non-important but it is important

Where does your mind wonder

when it's not calculating?

When you aren't occupied with the next move

The next paycheck next month's rent,

If you can afford the medical test you need

Where does your mind go if allowed to be free?

Free to figure out what it is you like

What to do with your spare time

What to do for fun, where to eat, how to dress?

The best part of finally living is finding out how

I often forget about our days when we were
long-distance; a six-hour drive separated me from
your touch. I couldn't see you whenever I wanted.
I couldn't talk to you whenever I wanted. I would lie
awake with my heart aching to be near you. I would
wonder if your heart was aching, too?

Everybody would ask how we did it. How we
stayed together for three years, never once breaking
up with the distance between us. I always had the
same response, "What's one more year if we are
going to spend the rest of our lives together?"

The juxtaposition of motherhood is startling

It draws families closer together

and pulls friendships apart

I am never alone physically,

yet I am completely emotionally alone

I miss my old life, my career, and my friends

But how do I treasure these babies

more than my own life?

How do both of these statements stand to be true?

Motherhood is for tortured souls, and yet these

children make me whole

My heart is full, and my body is tired

Motherhood is nuanced, complicated,

beautiful, and rewarding

I would go through all this again to see their

smiling faces

We act upon our feelings

They rule our decisions, acting as our true north

We use them as guides leading our way

When in fact, our feelings were made to deceive us

A camouflaged snake, waiting in the grass

Ready to strike, given any proximity

When the true act of courage is going

against your feelings

Deciding what you know to be consistent

Just and fair

It may as feel as though you are betraying yourself

When for the first time,

you are being true to yourself

You are being rational and secure

When you aren't relying on feelings

Which are fleeting and unpredictable to

direct your path

You can begin to forge a new one,

clear of snakes and debris

I always have so many emotions on Good Friday. I can typically express my emotions by written word much more than spoken word. This year, with the world in shambles, I am at a complete loss for words, written and spoken. Not because there isn't anything to say about Good Friday, but maybe because there is so much to say about Good Friday. Holy Week is a reflective time for me and Christians around the world. The heaviness that Jesus was celebrated, betrayed, and crucified within a week lies on my heart. The physical and emotional pain He experienced so that I may go to Heaven in all my brokenness, mistakes, and failures is a concept I am not sure I fully and truly comprehend.

I love this holiday. It marks the coming of warmer weather, the showing of spring, and a reminder that all the living things that died, much like Jesus are coming back to life. It's symbolic that Easter is in the Spring, showing you that when you seek shelter in His name, no matter how dormant you have become, He can bring you back to life.

Stay well friends

Walk away from things and people that aren't

serving you or your family

Time cannot be purchased, traded, or exchanged

Have the hard conversations

Close the doors and open new ones

Do the work

Find your way back

Be brave

Be scared

Be uncomfortable

Be you

I was waiting when I met you.

I was waiting for you not to respond
To tell me the long distance was too much
Waiting for you to fall out of love with me
I thought you would recite a million reason why I
wasn't the one
I waited for you to find someone better
You kept me waiting for these things to happen.
But while I waited
You showed up
You called when you said you would
You loved on me
You were consistent
You were dependable
You were good

I know your words fail you often, but my love
Your actions spoke louder than words
And, I've always been able to hear them
loud and clear
Your actions told me to stop waiting, so I did

I have made a decision

No more self-help books or podcasts

No more social media influencers

I am done trying to fix something that isn't broken

I am created in His likeness and perfect image

I need to learn how to sit with myself in order to be

the best version of myself

I need to quiet the background noise that is

constantly playing in my mind

If I don't know myself, then who else will?

How will I know who I am if I'm constantly trying

to change her?

12.31

The pressure to look back is so painful,
I can't explain why.
I search for what filled my days as time rushed by
This yearly renewal is a reminder that nothing was
renewed, only maintained
My heart aches, and I can't help but feel ashamed

Everyone is a year older
Anniversaries are a year longer
I survived each day
hoping to only make me stronger
The days became weeks,
and the weeks became months
And before long, time is only
measured in accomplishments

Day in and day out, I have shown up as a mother,
wife, friend, and daughter.
I should not be embarrassed;
I should only applaud her

And today, a day made for reflection,

I have decided that contentment is my new direction

I am convinced that women hold

all their power in their hair

When we need more confidence or feeling sad

We change our hair—the color, the cut, the length...

It brings men to their knees

I can decide to wear it up or down, straight or curled

It depends on my mood and

how much control I want

I can play with it in a meeting

I can decide how this is going to go

When I'm feeling flirty or serious

Or when I need to just feel like myself

I can do all this just from my hair

Journal Entry: June 2021

I listened to a CEO today on a Zoom call. The only thing that I could think of was I wished I could go back and tell that little girl inside of me that you really are smarter than most people. Everyone is making this up, and these people just got lucky; they are mostly idiots. I wish I could tell her to stick it out; whatever she wanted to do, she could do it. The most incompetent people are in the highest positions, seriously. They just believed in themselves more than you did/do. Imagine where I would be if had known this in college. I can't think about it, it pisses me off and just makes me jealous.

I have these skeletons lying around

A graveyard marked with stones

Past versions of myself that continue to haunt me

One by one, I can see them trying to rise

I can feel them searching for the life they once had

But how do I let these bones lie?

And keep them buried until they turn to dust?

How do I ignore all these versions that had to die

In order to become my true self

Perhaps I should dance with these skeletons and

embrace who I once was

Perhaps it's through death we can only begin to live

I shall mark the gravestones

for when I need to visit them

Calling them out by name

A gentle reminder to me that I am not the same

We had to fall apart; don't you see?

There were cracks, leaks, and weak spots

The only way to save us was to start over

How else could we have put it all back together?

Even better than it was before

If the moon is powerful enough to change the tides
of the ocean, imagine what it can do to us.
We are mostly water after all.

Christmas Eve

There is something about a dark, still room, singing
Silent Night by candlelight that gets me every time.
I'm a sucker for this man named Jesus. His presence
draws me in every time
His perfect, calming, loving, reassuring,
faithful presence
Remember when the world is dark and cold around
you, today and everyday
God sent his Son to earth to be our
light and warmth.
December 25th is just a date on a calendar
A date to represent the darkest day of the year so we
may celebrate the light being sent to us,
in our darkest hour.
Christmas can be busy, heavy, and feel burdensome
Take a moment to reflect on the stillness and
calmness that Christmas was meant to be

Thriving

It took me thirty-nine years to find my voice. Now,
I must learn how to use it.

The most beautiful I have ever felt are the times I've been growing humans inside of me. Creating life is my favorite thing to do. How lucky am I that I have gotten to grow three.

Lucille

In a sea of princesses, be the dragon.

Stay Fierce, my girl.

The world is waiting for you.

Judith

You healed the parts of your dad that I wounded.
He needed you
I wanted you
We all love you

Candler

You were sent to heal my broken heart and change
the course of our lives forever. My sweet boy, your
smile lights up every room you are in, never lose
that smile.

In the end, I don't want a life well lived.

I want them to say, what a life well loved.

I remember so many vivid details of that day as
If, they happened just yesterday.

And some details I have absolutely no recollection
of. It's astonishing to me how so many memories of
such an important event can be lost to trauma and
time. But in the end, the only details that matter are
that my daughter is alive, and so am I.

NICU

Air runs through tubes breathing life into you
Taped wires
Beeping screens
Flashing numbers
No medicine can save you
Only the fight within you

Mothers are helpless
Doctors can't heal
You can only depend on yourself
How bad do you want to be here with us?
The look of pain that I can't see
All of this is beyond my control

I want you here so badly
I whisper in your ear
My body created you
But couldn't keep you safe
I'm so sorry
I'm so sorry

I'm so sorry

I need you to understand

THIS was not the plan

How cruel of a world

Mothers can't fix their child's pain

Each day, I watch you choose life

I witness your fight

I'm already in awe of your strength

May you carry that strength with you

all the days of this life

Sometimes I find it hard to breathe

Your love is so suffocating

Not that there is anything wrong with you

I just feel like I'm drowning

I have never treaded in waters this deep before

Your love is fierce

Unconditional, unwavering

Over time, I've dipped my toes in the water

Slowly submerging myself with each step

Teaching myself to swim in your depth

For these waters are warm and calm and

healing my soul

I am a water sign after all

As soon as I find myself slipping

out of love with you again

I see the way our children light up in your presence

And I fall in love with you all over again

Ten Years

Ten trips around the sun

Ten years feels like a lifetime ago

And other times, it seems like yesterday

I have had the privilege of being loved by you for
fourteen years

And I'm still in awe of all the love you have to give

You love us so well, unconditionally, and fiercely

My favorite times are our most difficult times

The long distance, the difficult conversations

The tears, the IVF, the hospital visits,
the life-threatening deliveries

The NICU stays

The job losses and changes

Long days, and even longer nights

Because it was in these times

The most vulnerable of times

We came together and loved each other the most

Happy Anniversary, Love

I couldn't see the forest for the trees

The master plan, a divine design, created just for me

But the same Creator who said, I gave you this life

Also said to nurture it, water it, and give it light

As time passed and the fog lifted

I came to realize what I had been gifted

A life full of hope, love, and laughter

If I was courageous enough

to see the happily ever after

Life is on a grand scale

As long as we do not get lost in the detail

We can see that it is beautiful,

messy, and complicated

And it is not something that should be

taken for granted

I can't remember the last time

I laughed uncontrollably

The kind of laugh that brings tears to your eyes

The laugh that lights up your soul and

changes your chemistry

Life is heavy like that sometimes;

the joy is buried deep inside.

But if I am willing to wait, I know it ebbs and flows

And as sure as the sun rises each day

I will have a season of laughter again

Shoot for the moon and land among the stars....

I read this back, and I got angry with myself.

I question what made me

decide this was inspirational

It was as if I had already tied my hands

behind my back

Only hoping, wishing to reach the stars

When it was the moon calling to me, not the stars or

the earth below

The moon wanted me,

and I was too afraid to answer

I know now that it was well within reach

And I should have reached for her all along

How arrogant was I to think I did this on my own?

I had help
I found help in unlikely places and sometimes in
unfamiliar faces

I had luck
Luck is sometimes just good timing

I had love
I'm so deeply loved by family and friends

I had forgiveness
Each time I screwed up, I was given grace

I had grit
A perseverance I inherited from my grandmother

I had faith
Complete confidence and trust in God
and a master plan

And yet, I still thought I did this alone.

I showed you the ugliest parts of me,

and you still stayed.

You didn't wonder or waiver, not even once

You met my family and loved me anyway

I overshare and overindulge

In response, you just love me more

I've hurt you in my wake

You didn't even flinch

You loved me when I was insecure

and too opinionated

When I was sorry for being too loud and too smart

You told me not to be

When I was too much, you didn't go find less

I have to at least try to shatter these glass ceilings

I have to at least try to begin all this healing

I have to at least try to make sure

I have a seat at this table

I have to at least try to prove that I am able

I have to at least try to find my voice

I have to at least try to make sure girls are rejoiced

I have to at least try, even if it is shocking

I have to at least try, my daughters are watching

I look around at all that I have and gratefulness
seeps from every pore of my body.
Most times, it escapes through my eyes
in the form of tears.

I wear my heart on my sleeve times three

Three hearts beat outside my body

Three little people who are mine to love and protect

Triple the chances of having my heart broken

Their little hearts are so fragile yet so full of love

I get the love I give back times three

How do you love me so well?

The real question is

Why do you love me so well knowing

I can't love you as much?

I can't love you as much as you love me

The amount of love you have to give

will always be a mystery to me

How lucky are we, those that get to be loved by you

Thank you for loving me despite only being able to

return a fraction of what you give

I am not the same person that I was at twenty-five
when we met.

I've grown, matured, lived,
and parts of me have died
I've felt security and safety for the first time
In my life
It changed and transformed me,
parts of me are now alive

What comes with this new version of me
A version that I am unfamiliar with
One that doesn't just survive
but one that is trying to find out
Who should I have been all along?

I don't know who this person is
or what to do with her
But I'm determined to find out

Thank you for reading my stories, my words, and my heart. I have wanted to write a book for so long, and I never could figure out exactly which story I wanted to tell; I had so many. Turns out, poetry allowed me to tell all of my stories. I hope you find the words inspiring, encouraging, healing, and comforting. Most importantly, I hope these words meet you where you are in life. I hope they remind you that you are not alone, that human experiences are universal regardless of what you look like and where you come from, we are all in life together.